Two Cats in the Yard

Two Cats in the Yard

Poems by

Lin Nelson Benedek

© 2025 Lin Nelson Benedek. All rights reserved.
This material may not be reproduced in any form, published,
reprinted, recorded, performed, broadcast,
rewritten or redistributed without
the explicit permission of Lin Nelson Benedek.
All such actions are strictly prohibited by law.

Cover design by Shay Culligan
Cover image by Zhang Kaiyv on Unsplash
Author photo by Tom Benedek

ISBN: 978-1-63980-772-7

Kelsay Books
502 South 1040 East, A-119
American Fork, Utah 84003
Kelsaybooks.com

This book is dedicated to all those affected by the fires
in Altadena and Pacific Palisades, including our
precious wildlife and community cats, indoor and out.
May our sweet towns rise from the ashes
and become more beautiful than ever.

Acknowledgments

I would like to thank the publications in which versions of these poems first appeared:

Beir Bua: "Read Me"

Quartet Journal: "Musings of an Okay Poet of the 21st Century" (Pushcart Prize nominee)

Lyrics from Graham Nash's "Our House" provide the five cozy words which serve as the title of this book.

Gratitude always to my magnificent mentors and professors at Pacific University for initiating me into the brave and beautiful world of poetry—Kwame Dawes, Anna Journey, Dorianne Laux, Joseph Millar, Vievee Francis, David St. John, Marvin Bell, and Ellen Bass.

I would like to thank Susan Hayden and Alexis Rhone Fancher for their brilliance and generosity as writers and as friends and for welcoming me so graciously into the LA poetry community. I would also like to thank Alexis for her stellar editorial skills, which have served to deepen and enliven my work.

Deepest love and appreciation to my treasured family, friends, poetry sisters and brothers and teachers.

To darling Yuka for bringing so much love and joy into our lives.

Tommy and Nicky—forever—my heart and my soul.

Contents

I

Long-Married	17
Your Hands	18
Madly in Love	20
Thirst for Knowledge	22
Some Women Write Books	23
Musings of an Okay Poet of the Twenty-First Century	24
Ars Poetica	27
In My Defense, Your Honor, I Was Drunk on Words	28
Self-Portrait with Interruptions	29

II

You with Your Tintoretto Eyes	35
Read Me	39
Wood Turner	40
You'll Know It When You See It	41
You Don't Choose Your Soul, My Soul	42
Solace	43
Tree Spirits	45
Five Weeks with our Five-Year-Old in London Town	46

III

Dreamer, Your Dreams	51
A Dairy Maid Can Milk Cows to the Glory of God	52
Goldilocks	58
Left and Right	59
Construction	60

Bendinelli vs. Guerrero   65
Life and Other Maladies   66

IV

Two Cats in the Yard   71
Poetry   74
Blind Faith   80
Mountain View   81
A Long Way to Rarotonga   84
When the Light Breaks Over You   86
Maybe You Can Go Home Again   87
Unrule This Ruly Paradise   88

Perhaps home is not a place but simply an irrevocable condition.
—James Baldwin

I

Long-Married

after Joseph Millar's "Sole Custody"

Today the old man tends his seedlings. The dirt teems with life, and he's moving heaven and earth, piling bags onto the wheelbarrow—worm casings, chicken manure, crustacean shells—in the fading light. He hasn't taken a break for hours. He's twisted tendrils of snow peas and snap peas onto the trellis netting; carted load after load of river stones to make a path to the raised beds. I ease into the worn leather chair and, when he comes in, register weariness on his face. He shows me the callouses on his hands. I love this man. I love these hands. The screensaver dolphins are back. Gray blue swimmers in a blue gray sea. I could be more relaxed. *Do you ever wish you were with one of your old boyfriends?* he asks. We're a couple of astronauts, hurtling through space in our shared capsule. We're Thing One and Thing Two. I'm Old Mother Hubbard and he's the Farmer in the Dell. *Sit down with me,* I say. *I thought you'd never ask,* he replies. One of us will fall asleep in the chair while we watch TV. We stay up too late for a couple of septuagenarians. The doctor scolds us like children. But we'll never change. This is our time. We don't want it to end.

Your Hands

after Dorianne Laux's "Your Face"

    The major motion picture of your open palms
Peaked Himalayas of your roughed-up knuckles
Cooing doves of your hands in repose
Your bare hand on my thigh

    Opposable prizefighter thumbs
Baryshnikov grace of index finger
Hoary forest bed on the back of the hand
Stand up and be counted veins

    Glorious wreckage of ten nailbeds
Sassy backtalk of middle finger
Ooh Baby of your Magic 8 Ball touch
Bengal tiger of sinews in motion
Crouching tiger of the hand in a fist

    Fierce independence of naked ring finger
Weed scent on first joints of thumb and pointer
Fleshy kiss of your fingertip

    Touchy-feely hands
Dig in the garden hands
Swift ratatat of typing hands

    Press the crust in the pie pan hands
Lift the baby to the sky hands
Hypnotize the cat and dog with your touch hands
Fold the receipt neatly
and put it in your wallet hands

    Your good-with-your-hands hands
Your hands can do anything hands
Your chips on the table, all in, hands
Your finger on the trigger
Your hand in mine

Madly in Love

*If these delights thy mind may move,
Then live with me and be my love.*
   —Christopher Marlowe

Yesterday, a beautiful surprise.
Our son is marrying Yuka,

from Tokyo. Before bed
he called. Yuka's mom

cried when she heard the news.
Tears of happiness? I asked.

She and I
would have arranged this marriage

in another time and place. A psychic
from Jakarta pronounced them soulmates.

They are perfect. The lovebirds brought
souvenirs from a friend's wedding

in Tepotzlan: tiny gourd painted green
and pink, small bird tapestry, sombrero

keychain made of clay, turtle refrigerator
magnet. At the farmer's market

near the train stop in South Pasadena,
sunflowers for the mantel. The lovers

are coming. I want everything to be beautiful.
I want to be beautiful, but settle for kind,

helpful, friendly. Tom is cooking fish
for dinner, and soba. Yuka's mom picked out

the noodles. Yuka brought them from Japan.
Every day I pray. May this love be lasting.
May this love be true.

Thirst for Knowledge

A visit to my college campus, fifty years on—a great place for love, requited and non. Twenty-one fountains. Eighteen courtyards. Edible plants, fruit and olive trees. At the college art gallery, flowers and birds in Japanese art of the seasons, on woodblocks, kimonos and inro. Chrysanthemums for fall. Bamboo, ginko, red maple. Snow for winter; snow-covered pine. Bush warblers and flowering plum for spring. Wisteria for love and endurance. For summer, monsoon season, sun, rain and the cuckoo for longing. Deep purple irises. Peonies, the queen of flowers, for feminine beauty, depicted with lions. In the rare book room, a cuneiform tablet, 2000 BCE; an illuminated manuscript of the *Book of Hours;* a page from the *Gutenberg Bible;* a book inscribed to the library by Langston Hughes on his visit in 1939. *The Whole Art of Hairdressing* from 1792. A rare photograph of Sojourner Truth. Music from the Christian calendar year depicting plants and insects from the spring season. (No *Kama Sutra* in Sanskrit on palm leaves, but I can dream.) Back home I greet the Engelman oak. In the evening we watch Elle King and Miranda Lambert on YouTube: *I got some new best friends forever, see I met 'em at a bar.* I wish I had their guts. And their chops. Last night I was back in the dorm again, in my dream. There is always more to learn.

Some Women Write Books

Some women are books.
Some books are women,
swept up on the beach
written by water.
Some books are water,
written from memory
in the shape of oceans.
Some women are oceans
dreaming books they will
someday write. Some
women are oceans
dreaming lives they will
someday live.

Musings of an Okay Poet of the Twenty-First Century

with a line from Wallace Stevens

1.
Lady and the Tramp introduced me to love.
My love is three weeks older, four inches taller.
I admit I am a bit like Glinda. I discovered boys
before they discovered me.

2.
How to make guests feel comfortable in your poem: Give them something to pluck. My literary companions: the Jabberwocky, some rough beast, dappled things, little red feet of the pigeons.

3.
Dreams are common property, someone said. And something resembling sorrow. One friend sends me peacocks; another, butterflies. And here is my pantheon of old boyfriends, gods all. See how the scars define me.

4.
Stars can't be all bad. Nor flowers, trees, birds and bees. And anyway, most of us are mutts.

5.
Turn on the radio and never turn it off. Listen with eyes that hear, hands that breathe, taste that deciphers smell.

6.
Meanwhile, another rattlesnake dream, empty and holy. And an experience which shall remain nameless. To the poet in me, hereinafter called the artist: What shall I write about today? Culinary banquet? Prurient debauch? Pastoral tableau? Nautical voyage? Surefire tearjerker? Unfettered joy?

7.
Moonday through Aphrodite Day:
Coax the inchoate from its cloak of invisibility.
Did someone else say this, or did I?

8.
Fall poem: fall in line, fall of man, fall asleep, fall in love

9.
Be free. Be strong. Be Beautiful. (Buzz words on FM 98.1)

10.
Eros *and* Thanatos?

11.
I was always a character actor, just born with the looks of Little Red Riding Hood, said Paul Newman. I had a brush with greatness as a waitress at Viva Zapata in Westport, Connecticut, when I showed Paul Newman the way to the men's room. The sky was cornflower blue and cloudless, like his eyes, no hint of artifice.

12.
O, rueful moon! I have reached my dew point. Japanese scientists have created a mutant mouse that does not fear cats. But can they make a man with no enemies? I count on the curve of the duck's head in profile, the duck's back, his sense of comedy. The dog keeping time with tongue and tail. And a 1500-year-old Byzantine church with a well-preserved mosaic floor and images of lions, foxes, fish, and peacock.

13.
Does it hurt when the leaves begin to turn?

14.
Notes for a poem with sparrows: *Light Plight Bright Height Might Flight*

15.
To be continued. *The blackbirds singing, or just after.*

Ars Poetica

A few feathers
A ton of bricks
Considerable rocks
A big grin
A lot of grit
Joy, pain, an inside joke or two
Plain words and fancy
Bees, butterflies, both or neither
A punch in the gut
Music, sonorous or tripping
A change of heart
A flash of truth
A bucket of sorrow
A heart on a sleeve
Crow of the rooster, cluck of the hen
Part contrivance, part wonder
Part pawnshop and part patisserie
Mostly song and one part prayer
Shaggy and ragtag or buttoned-down
Spare or rambling, depending
Part sage, part buffoon, part preacher
Part teacher, part stripper
Too big for its britches
Part doubt and part faith
Part gingerbread, part opium
Part teacup, part star

In My Defense, Your Honor, I Was Drunk on Words

Wrecked, out for the count, smashed, canned, sloshed, bombed, plastered, hammered, wasted, tanked, juiced, fried, cooked. Drunk and disorderly. Black-out drunk. The stages of my inebriation.

My tongue became fluent in many tongues: Blue ball blue bell blue bowl bon mot crash course hob nob two step ground swell hip hop speed bump road kill hand bill speed ball curve ball free fall slip shod.

I lost all control: Ship shape riff raff hot shot low blow heart ache back bend fire storm punch line junk mail bear hug land mine land line cash crop cash flow cash cow.

I confess: crow flies fire sale sure fire know how firefly flash back blow back live wire flat line code blue no clue back talk back hoe short hand word play speed boat dream boat.

I threw in some furry bees. For the buzz. For the honey. For pheromones of flowers. For recollection of a sting. And a Biblical reference for good measure (e.g., *Gethsemane*) and the effing ineffable.

See how we spew: Tipsy. Under the influence. Blotto, trashed, thrashed, lit.

Self-Portrait with Interruptions

I
Oh, to be a swan. A mean swan on a lake in France. I have only the regrets I can remember.

II
Dad had secrets, and I don't mean the obvious ones—the women, the drinking. I'm talking about the quiet things. The early shyness; thin skin to go with the freckles and red curls. The secret longing to be soothed. His unrequited need for Mom. When he was born his mother said, *I don't care if it's a rabbit. I'll keep it.* She had three older boys but her baby girl died at birth a year before Don (my dad) came along. My grandmother once famously dressed him as Little Bo Peep. She tutored and coached his three school-smart brothers. But not Don, who did well in life but not in school. How he craved the respect of his brothers. How he loved us when we were little. We knew he was coming by the jingle of coins in his pocket. I liked the jingle. He liked the green gum with the chlorophyll. Clorets. I smelled it on his breath. I might have been a Daddy's girl, but Mom wouldn't have it. She painted flowers. They weren't realistic enough to please my dad. The triangular version is this: we were all just trying to survive.

III
The boy-craziness wasn't all fun and games. It felt close to love when they touched me that way. My vagina was never far from my thoughts. Even back then I could count on it to alert me to danger, provide clues to my whereabouts, soothe my troubled nerves when nothing else could.

IV

Set me loose, like Diane Seuss, who conjures with scale and travels wide. If I were free, like Diane Seuss, I would tell you anything: a mystery unsolved. Like that time in my earliest twenties when I blacked out and, next morning, could not remember to save my life whether or not I'd slept with the bartender. How I confided in my sweet friend Russ, the cook, who said, *Do you want me to ask him?* And how I said, *Oh, God, no.*

V

Poppycock, Fiddlesticks, the elders used to say. Poets and they didn't know it.

VI

Jealousy: Feed it scraps and it will grow stronger, linger longer. It will shame you, aim its nasty barbs at you and blame you. If you can't let it go, make a cozy space for it in the quiet of your becoming. Tame it. Name it—something approachable, like Cinderella or Dulcinea. When it starts to act up, give it gingerbread and tea.

VII

The mountains this morning are a shaggy beast, nothing questionable about them.

VIII

If it's fun, it's wrong, Dad always said. *Do as I say, not as I do,* Dad never said. This old man had a whole ton of fun. Smoking is fun. Drinking is fun. Sex is fun. A whole lot of sex is a whole lot of wrong. *Do as I say, not as I do,* Dad never said. So I did what he did.

IX
Everyone at the table ordered a different kind of pie. You never know what will change your life: an outside table for seven at the Village Kitchen Pie Shoppe in Carlsbad—all it was cracked up to be—Key Lime, Boston Cream, Dutch Apple, Oregon Blackberry, Gooseberry Fool, Georgia Peach, New York Cheesecake—in what we mistook for the dwindling days of a global pandemic. I lied. I said it was my stepmother's ninetieth birthday.

X
Some days I hate myself. Our new neighbor, a Labradoodle, licked me immediately, so I can't be all bad.

XI
Our neighbor to the south dropped off the hot sauce she'd made. Hot but not too hot. I said *I need to rein in my effusiveness.* She said *No. No, you don't. We can all be droll and understated when we're dead.*

XII
Tell someone you love them.

II

You with Your Tintoretto Eyes

I
Gauguin gumption. Rembrandt cheekbones. Michelangelo hands. We are more Lucy and Ricky than George and Gracie. More Donald and Daisy than Desdemona and Othello. More Fred and Wilma than Mickey and Minnie. More Victoria and Albert than Marie Antoinette and Louis. Less Steve and Edie. More Adam and Evie. We are taking our sweet time. You can change my expression by touching me. A gardenia flutters in the region of my esophagus. Harpsichord strings vibrate in the belly of my muscles. I will love you in the next world and the next and the next.

II
Travelers, we are not strangers to carry on push back arrive at the gate first in line for take-off locked and upright position seatbelts securely fastened please refrain from smoking in the lavatory keep the aisles clear if you require assistance press the call button an attendant will assist you. I have loved you north, south, east and west. I'm remembering that shop in the Marais, *La Grenouille* and the Something Something, where we bought the illustration—*Les Panneaux, Gazelles et Oiseaux*—which hangs on our bedroom wall. And the large *Chemins de Fer Algériens* poster in oranges and tans which hangs in your office, the one with the looming camel. And three vintage postcards of Parisian kittens. Later we sat at a café. In the photograph your old man raises his eyebrows and I'm leaning to one side with my head thrown back. Five years later we're back in Paris with our three-year-old, and after a long day and a train ride to and from Giverny and a tour of the house and gardens, he has an epic tantrum outside a café. I hold onto him and don't let go until both of us are utterly worn out, and then we have dinner at the *Closerie des Lilas* and he raises his glass and says, *We'll always have Paris.*

III
In Cairo a black and white government cab carries us through the Ramadan crowds to the Meridien Hotel, where we're asked to give up our passports overnight. A few days later at dawn we board the Air Sinai flight to Tel Aviv from an unmarked gate and ask to have our passports stamped on a separate paper. The Cairo Museum, the turrets on the mosques, the Nile, Jerusalem, the camels, the bazaar, the Stations of the Cross, the Dome of the Rock, the Wailing Wall. Everything moves us in this part of the world. In our rental car on the drive to Bethlehem, "Sexual Healing" plays on the radio. I buy a wooden nativity scene in the gift shop at Mary's Milk Grotto. A star marks the spot.

IV
On the flight from LA to Milano I crack open a set of CDs called *Italian in Three Months* and over the fourteen hours on the plane I learn to say *bon giorno* e *buona sera* e *buona note* and other basics and just enough pronunciation to sound good. At the Enoteca Pinchiori in Florence I hear one waiter say to another *Lei è Italiana*—She's Italian. I can order perfectly—*mandorla & carciofi & cavolfiore & melanzana & finocchio*. But out on the street I'm useless. I ask for directions and never understand the reply. We travel south. How happy are we beside a pool in Positano overlooking the Mediterranean eating a sandwich of ciabatta, buffalo mozzarella, perfect tomatoes, fresh basil, a drizzle of olive oil, the sun about to sink into the sea in the pink light.

V
One time our engine caught fire on a flight from LA to Detroit and we made an emergency landing in Denver, flying so close to the Rockies it almost seemed we could touch them. We were strangely unafraid.

VI
We could put a finger on the spinning globe and pack a compass and go. Leaving the Alexander Hamilton rest stop in Weehawken for the Lincoln Tunnel towards Stroudsburg, we pass Newark, heading towards my Stevens and Marsh ancestors' settling place near the Delaware Water Gap in the Blakely Woods, passing signs, on the way, to Parsippany. We have lunch at the Corner Café and you take pictures through the window of Autumn, our server, the one with the Princess Mononoke tattoo, taking coffee to a guy out on the street. When we get closer to our destination the sign says *Bridge to America.* It's sunset when we catch our first view of the falls. There's a rainbow, always a rainbow. We can see the Horseshoe Falls from our hotel. The next morning, on the *Maid of the Mists,* a hundred of us in the blue slickers they've given us, we don't want it to end. But it does and we get on the Rainbow Bridge and wait in line for the customs officer to wave us through.

VII
We're rushing to catch Judy Collins at the Café Carlyle from the Cloisters at the end of Manhattan. If we don't make it there by 6:30 we're out of luck and we consult with one of the guards, a kid from New Jersey, who looks like our nephew, and he tells us the quickest way, and we leave the grounds, hop on the bus to the first subway stop, take the A train to the C, the crosstown bus to Fifth, walk fast ten blocks to the hotel, make it with a minute to spare, get the last of the bar seats and Sharif, the bartender, who usually works at the Bemelmans Bar, introduces himself. I walk through the tearoom—half pasha's palace and half brothel—to the ladies' room to change into my good shoes. When I get back Sharif nods towards the man at the end of the bar and says *Boss, would you bring me a bottle of Parker's for that gentleman's Appletini?* We sit a while and Judy arrives and tells stories about her father's radio

show and sings a song with lyrics from "Lake Isle of Innisfree" and reminisces about her recent trip to Ireland. She ends the evening with "Somewhere Over the Rainbow"—she was named for Judy Garland—and invites everyone to sing along, which in this small room means something.

VIII
A few weeks later, back home again, we're at Royce Hall listening to Taj Mahal and Vieux Farka Touré. The next perfect day, we hike Temescal to the waterfall, three miles round trip from the car and back, slipping on river stones on the downward slopes. Families with little kids, college kids, couples, friends. Yellow flowers growing wild after the rain. Cool at the waterfall and hot on the climb down. Later, back home, you stroke my feet, knead them like bread with your strong hands.

IX
We've never been to Istanbul. We have had drinks in the Bordello Room at the House of Blues on Sunset and thought it half resembled an opium den.

X
Last Sunday at Callisto Tea House our server picked out pink teacups to go with the amber notes of the Peach Elixir tea and two peach macarons. Tiny teacups so the tea stays hot. I used to drink. I used to smoke. I was never much for drugs. When we fell in love did the moon make a road on the water? Could I live in a world without you in it?

Read Me

Read me loud
Read me like a
Read me cover to cover
Read my lips
Eyes, ears and hands
Don't believe everything you
Read and re-read me
Read me in bed, on a bus,
On a train, on a plane
Speed read me and read me slow
Read me every day of the week
Don't judge me by my
Don't put me down

Wood Turner

Stoney Lamar knows trees.
When he loses his balance
the trees keep him straight.
Stoney knows wood.
He can bend trees like rubber
or cut them like diamonds.
Trees inhabit his forest,
his workroom, his dreams.
He lives on stone fruit and tree nuts,
found his way with the lathe
and the turning wheel. When
asked his secret he says,
Listen to the wood.

You'll Know It When You See It

I tried big red sun after a fire.
I tried deep rosy peony and camellia.
I tried redhead. And marmalade cat.
My friend says everyone needs
a romantic red. And so I tried garnet,
scarlet, claret, aubergine's red cousin:
autumnal rust. I wanted it redolent:
Vermillion, Rudolph or redcoat, red flag,
Red Bull, fire engine red, red robin, *Red
Rover come over, Ready or not here I come.
My luv is like a red, red* red. I tried sassy,
sultry. I even tried siren. Until I settled
for a dustier, blushier shade. Faded brick
on a garden path, not flashy, dazzling,
or daring. Slow burn red. Late bloomer red.
Been through the wash too many times red.
A red that goes with iridescent sea, shimmering
sand, sky-blue sky. A hue that's taken some knocks.
A red that says *Come live with me and be my love.*
A red that's sadder, and wiser, like me.

You Don't Choose Your Soul, My Soul*

—*Renata Ferreira*

You don't have to guess which ones, the blossoms
And don't you know that hammers always break
Take heart the Pleiades haven't gone anywhere
My truest ardor is all danger and ecstatic
When the woman downstairs sings she is always sharp
Because your face is expensive
You are a subject I cannot exhaust
Think of your life without all those narcissistic traumas
I don't care, I bought some roses
I get lonesome when you're away
All I want to do is sleep

A poem stitched from one line each of a group of poems by Renata Ferreira—Portuguese writer who may or may not be real—received and recorded by poet and novelist Frank X. Gaspar.

Solace

I didn't dream
my mother was alive
and well or that my son
brought home
a young dog.

I didn't dream
there was a war
going on and we were
making plans to leave
this land.

I didn't dream
of tanks in the street
or a military parade.

I didn't dream
of my childhood home,
my first love, my second,
or my third.

I didn't dream
of transformation
or crises of faith.

I didn't dream
of constitutions,
inquisitions
or Greek tragedy.

I dreamed
a red origami bird
tacked to a wall
in an empty room,
signifying, signifying.

Tree Spirits

—after Ellen Bass

Sometimes I need to touch the pocked
surface of the lid, trace my finger

along indented images of grape leaves, tawny
patterns on the mottled-brown of burnt

wood. She would be surprised to know
how much I treasure the box she made

as a girl, my grandmother. This box
that holds her prized wooden chess pieces.

Sixteen pawns; four knights, rooks
and bishops; two kings and two queens.

The family traveled so much she might
have made it in Colorado, Nevada

or Sonora, Mexico. It puzzled me
when I was young how little distinction

she made between the living and the dead,
her mother as much with her as I.

I didn't know how I'd stand it—never
seeing my beloveds again, never holding them

in my arms. They are a velvet presence now.
Inside the lid, fire-etched by a young hand
around 1900: *Williemarie Hannon*

Five Weeks with our Five-Year-Old in London Town

I was instructed to give him two drops of Sudafed half an hour before takeoff but the dropper leaked and he wound up with a whole dropperful. I was worried and told the flight attendant we needed to get off the plane right away. She refused, but she did call the airport medics. We waited and waited but they never arrived. Finally an announcement came on asking if there was a doctor on board. A young German physician stepped forward. He'd just completed his residency at Tulane. He examined our boy and said his heart rate was way up and his pupils were dilated but thought it was okay for him to make the twelve-hour flight from LAX to Heathrow. Because of all this, we took off two hours late, and our fellow travelers were not happy, and to make it more dramatic we were traveling with my husband's boss (a movie producer), who was not pleased, and it was a night flight, and our boy was up all night and we sang quiet songs and read books and played games.

When we landed we caught a cab to Knightsbridge and checked into our flat at the Beaufort House and my husband went to work but our boy was hungry and I took him straight to McDonald's, where he consumed a chicken nuggets Happy Meal and then rushed outside to throw up in the dustbin, as they call it, although he felt more than fine right away, cheerful and full of energy, not the least bit tired. I cleaned him up and we set out on our day, aware that most flights and trips with him involved a bout or two of vomiting, which didn't faze him in the least, and I learned to roll up a spare dress to tuck into my purse just in case.

We went from there, and most days thereafter, to the Natural History Museum. There was not a reptile living or extinct that frightened him. But he was mortally afraid of the hominid exhibit. We'd hurry past while he held one hand over his eyes and the other hand in mine. That's when I fell in love with the dodo bird—life-sized replica of the large flightless bird from Mauritius Island, off the coast of Africa, in the Indian Ocean, extinct since around 1680. Wikipedia says the irresistible dodo, with his pale blue translucent eyes, was not dumb, just friendly and trusting; that when Dutch and Portuguese explorers landed on Mauritius the giant birds didn't bother to scatter; that they had no reason to fear other creatures until cats, dogs, rats and pigs came over with the sailors on ships; that they'd never had predators on the island, and the dodo was lost to us when forests were destroyed, cutting off their food supply, and creature stowaways destroyed their nests.

After the museum we'd stroll through the stalls of the food court at Harrod's for dinner provisions and sometimes we'd go upstairs to the toy department for a small book or Lego. After that we'd stop at the playground in Kensington Gardens and one day we toured the palace, where Diana and her boys were living then, Princes William and Harry, and while we were there our little prince had a piece of cake at the palace café and when we were leaving he threw up in the foyer of Princess Diana's palace. It turned out he had a tummy bug, as the doctor called it, Dr. Lefèvre, which they pronounced *Le Fever*, which our boy found hilarious because he did have a fever, and was for the first time in his five years delirious at times, waking us up in the night laughing an unfamiliar laugh in his sleep. I boiled potatoes for days, for his tummy, perfect potatoes from Harrod's, and sometimes in the afternoon my husband and the director would join us at the flat for Fortnum and Mason's Royal Blend tea with milk and McVitie's biscuits while our boy sat at the table drawing triceratopses and pterodactyls with red, green, blue and yellow markers. When our son was well again we made more trips to the Natural History Museum and the zoo, Buckingham Palace, the Tower of London, Westminster Abbey, Big Ben, the National Portrait Gallery, the Victoria and Albert Museum.

The night we left for the airport he fell asleep in the back of the old London cab, a little nap, meaning he'd be up all night on the long flight home and we'd be reading stories like *Whiskers and Rhymes* and *Old Possum's Book of Practical Cats* and *Frog and Toad*. We read the garden story twice. Frog tells Toad it takes time and patience for the seeds in his garden to grow. Toad listens to his friend's advice. He sings to his little plants, plays the violin for them and reads them stories and poems. To Toad's delight, his little plants grow strong.

III

Dreamer, Your Dreams

*—after Antonio Machado, with a line about dreams
inspired by Tony Hoagland*

Dreamer, you've had this dream before.

Another dream about X: Keke Palmer
wants you to get over yourself, in your dream.

Wear the damn dress, she says, *Wear all the bells
and let them ring.*

Jeff Beck's playing on Pandora:

"Cause We've Ended as Lovers."
Don't say

I wouldn't look fine in a Valkyrie
breastplate and braids.

Dreamer, what if there is no dream? Only

the surreal flicker of the 16 millimeter
movie that is your mind.

A Dairy Maid Can Milk Cows to the Glory of God

—Martin Luther

In the beginning . . .
—John 1:1

I
We chanted, meditated, hugged rocks and trees.
Went back inside, sat still and listened
to "Silence Is the Answer."

Heavy gongs conjured dark monasteries
and stirred old angers, but when the music changed
to flutes and bells all rancor left me.

It was the last day
of Mind and Body class at Pacific Oaks College, an all-day
retreat.

It was 1982. Classes like this were uncommon then
for psychotherapists-in-training. Some complained,
but I relished a day to know myself better.

II
I opened
my eyes and looked out the window. Rain

brought out the grays, greens and blues
over the clouded arroyo. Next we listened

to "Sounds of Morning." Jungle sounds,
and my thoughts leapt to Gracie and Montana, our cats

at home, and their rapt excitement in the presence
of birds. I imagined the unfolding of plants

and flowers, cells renewing themselves with life and health.
I sensed my mother's spirit in the music, in the unseen circle

of humming, buzzing eternity. No fear.
One road back:

being here, allowing love.
The sound of a rooster's crows on the recording

rooted me to the ground where I sat.

III
We wrote
intentions on slips of paper. Set the slips

on fire and let the smoke carry them on the wind. We
danced around a tree and played simple instruments.

Danced in a spiral to Baroque music. Touched seashells
and bathed our hands in a container of water with rose petals

floating on top; dried our hands in the sun and studied
a camellia, two shades of pink, in a blue and white bowl.

The leaves were strong and green with a delicate underside
in a lighter, veinier shade. The wrapper layers were a pale hue

and the base of the flower formed a casing for the pink petal
layers above.

IV
Our teacher read a passage from Aldous Huxley:

*Our goal is to discover that we have always been where we ought
to be.*

She said: *We are all one with the infinite sun. The earth, the wind,
the fire, the rain. Return Return Return Return.*

We got quiet. And still. And listened. Mined memories
of childhood. Trees, bushes, flowers, wet grass, wood floors,
picture books, dominoes and chessmen, bare feet, footsteps, braids,
furry animals.

We talked about *Machina* (lists, files, clocks, noise, worries, plans,
too much to do, getting ready) and *Mandala* (circle, wholeness).
We talked about neurotransmitters

and chakras. Meditating upon the *Mandala* I saw a lotus flower,
water lilies,
a globe of light. I pictured a stream, water surging over stones,
gathering sticks

and other debris and flowing on unobstructed and our teacher asked:
Where do we end? Where does the world begin?

She said:

*Catch the wave of your breath.
Bring kindness into your awareness
in each successive moment.*

V

We meditated upon a second passage from Huxley:

*If the doors of perception were cleansed everything would appear
to man as it is, infinite.*

I imagined my senses housed in a fuse box the size of a small
 room.
I swept and dusted and wiped it down. My eyes were a movie
 camera.

I cleansed the lenses with cotton balls and lemon juice. My ears
 were
an old Victrola, the RCA dog looking on. I cleansed the horn with
 Q-tips

and fresh rags. Sense of smell was a hound dog sniffing. He
 splashed
and bathed in fresh water and shook the water off.

Taste was an elephant with a giant tongue. I scrubbed his tongue
with a long-handled brush and sprayed him down with a garden
 hose.

Touch was a pleasure dome decorated with Persian rugs, fans,
 palms.
I dusted with a long-handled feather duster, shook out the rugs,
swabbed down octagonal mosaic tiles. Intuition was a control room
 with curved walls,

a computer terminal, complex and intricate. I cleaned and I
 cleaned,
working closely in small areas, dusting wires and other parts with a
 soft

white cloth. And then I swept the floor. When I opened my eyes I
 took in the red patterned rug and my classmate's therapy dog, a
 Golden Retriever.

I thought of the hound dog

in my reverie, of his self-cleaning mouth, his long nose. Noise was
 coming from the kitchen. In my heightened state the clatter
 of pots and pans sounded like bells. I was aware
of the velvet pillows beneath me. I thought of Scheherazade
and the pleasure dome of my imaginings.

VI

Our teacher recited another chant:

Listen, listen, listen to my heart's song.
Listen, listen, listen to my heart's song.

I will never forget you. I will never forsake you.
I will never forget you. I will never forsake you.

Listen, listen, listen to my heart's song.

VII

We ended the day with a last meditation to music:
"The First Time Ever I Saw Your Face,"
the original, sung by Roberta Flack.

I dared to ask the biggest question.

Why am I here?

The answer came, I swear. It was simple.

To love and be loved and to love the world.

I'd always known it, but hadn't known I'd known it—
not until there were words.

Goldilocks

They said you were
too quiet, Goldilocks.
And too loud.
Too neat and too messy.
Too fancy and too plain.

Goldilocks, they said you were
too greedy. Too generous, lazy
and hardworking; too fat and too
thin. Too shy and too bold, too
young and too old.

They said you were too rich
and too poor. Too much
and not enough.

And then, Goldilocks, once
upon a glorious time, you said
No. I'm quite sure I'm just right.

Left and Right

Mommy is dying. I will be twenty and this will be my last birthday
    with her in it.
I ask for two parting gifts from my precious mother. A rocking
    chair, for solace;
and leather boots, for one foot in front of the other. What I really
    want is for her
not to die. We find a bentwood rocker at Pier One. It has a cane
    seat and back
and a black wooden frame. We find the boots at Huggins on South
    Lake. They are tan,
supple, soft, mid-calf height, each with a thin leather strap to wrap
    around the vamp
like the ties on a Grecian gown. I meant to keep the boots forever
    but outgrew them
after our son was born. I became a mother ten days after I turned
    forty. If I had my way,
the rocker would come with me when I die.

Construction

The Bobcat operator readies his mechanical
beast. This hotshot's from Ace Demolition,

and this is his derby and this his agile battering ram,
more bull-elephant than beast, more beast

than bobcat. Model S185 pulls back for runway space,
pauses a second, barrels in, breaks down walls,

rips the roof off like Godzilla. Pounds and pummels
tan stucco crush. A nihilist's dream.

At the remaining edge of the structure, piles
of redwood, lath, and plaster rubble.

Remains of the garage,
built close to a century ago at the end of a long

driveway, to hold a 1926 Chrysler Imperial.
We're clearing a spot for a tiny house for our son

and his beloved. Deodars and mountains to the north.
Towering palms to the south and east. Massive Coast

Live Oak and rosy sunsets to the west. But back
to the wrecking crew, and our Bobcat driver.

Watch him barrel in, crush wooden
beams, bash in walls, break up concrete, and pulverize

debris with the swing arm spear. Brutal basher,
jackhammer rhythm of the wrecking tools and tight jerky

turns and reverses, and then more black, more red,
more tan detritus. Isn't it a thrill sometimes, to tear it
all down? Is it wrong to relish such destruction?

Surveyors take measurements and mark the boundaries, leave
    tracks
in old dirt where the garage used to be.

When it's time to break ground the excavation crew comes in with
    a small
John Deere tractor. Wildly it moves, sideways, on army-tank
    treads, swivels to open its jaws for giant bites of earth.

The next crew comes in with a cement mixer and pours
        the concrete. Teams stand
in the muck in high rubber boots getting rid of bubbles, framing
        the material with wooden

borders so it will dry and form a solid foundation; smoothing out
    the surface and squaring off the edges before it hardens and
    dries.

Framers arrive with sawhorses and lumber for studs, joists and
    crossbeams. Good wood: Doug Fir. And plywood for sheathing.

Walls go up. The roof comes on. And then drywall, electrical and
    plumbing.
The plumbers are the jolliest bunch. They bring a small barbeque
    and dine together.

Laughter, and lively music from La Raza, KLAX-FM. They make it look easy, digging trenches and laying down pipe. Earth piles up on either side of the deep furrows

they've dug. *Gravity's always better*, the architect says.
I'm learning a new language. The contractor uses words I don't know.

Cat wire spool. Crimp on. Stub it off. Punch list.
The electricians lay down the conduits.

And then stucco, the trickiest job.
Eventually it's time for the paint chip blues. What will it be? Duck Pond or

Restless Sea? Ebb Tide or Trinidad? If my childhood were a color it would be all the blues. Ultraviolet, aquamarine, somber navy, bright

turquoise, all those and more. At first I can't decide. But I settle on Duck Pond. (I'm nothing without a duck. I'm nothing without blue.)

Scalloped corbels, a pair, one for each front post, a small whoop-de-doo for the entrance. A flourish. Enough but not too much. And the balustrade, all about proportion.

The little house will have everything. Running water, a front porch, a romantic balcony. A back deck. Even a barbeque. Electric lights. Solar power. WiFi. Fruit trees.

A Moroccan pouf. A working toilet. Three fern pines. Vintage
    haute couture in the IKEA wardrobe. Vegetable beds. A view
    of fireworks in July. A garden arch. A cat

named Cha Cha, a dilute calico. Two turntables and a microphone.
    Dashi and bonito flakes in the red oak cupboards, for making
    soup. Honey from Enrique's hives,

his bees so trusting they never sting. A couple in love
in the morning light.

After the blue wheelbarrow and yellow ladder are gone, and
    the green tarp on the sawhorse, the pallet of leftover terracotta
    tiles, there will be trees. Buddha's

pine and olive; there will be roses, blue hibiscus, catmint and
    lavender. A white bird of paradise in the jade green pot from
    Mimi's. We are counting the days until the kids

come home. I think they'll like the view from halfway up
    the stairs, looking out onto the tile rooftops,
mountain ridges and tall palms.

I can see their house from my desk when I swivel around in the
    chair. When they're not in Tokyo they will be our nearest
    neighbors. Spring and Fall in Japan. Winter and Summer in
    California.

We didn't know at first whether we'd get a permit to build because
    of the Coast Live Oak on the neighbor's side of the wall. But
    the permit came through.

Once the excavation was complete the crew watered down the few
    stray roots, wrapped them in burlap and built a little house
    around them—permeable to let the nutrients in and keep them
    safe and train them

to grow downward so we could build up and do no harm. We've
    come to know the oak in all its seasons. The acorns are the first
to go.

Then the deep green leaves with their prickly edges, before they
    turn light brown. And when all the pollen has fallen,

the furry yellow catkins cascade in strands and crumble on my hat
    and clothes. Today the rain comes down steady. Sound bounces
    brightly as large

drops hit the metal gutter. It's the last day of September, but today
    is tomorrow
in Japan, and the tree has never looked happier. The outdoor cats
    think we built

the little house for them. Scaredy-cat Charlie, king of the jungle,
    sharpens his claws
on the welcome mat; marks his territory by the front door.

Bendinelli vs. Guerrero

The sound was off on the TV but the caption read
Barcelona Poker Championship
and I was too tired to get up and change the channel.

I watched Bendinelli take the million-plus pot
as he sweated bullets and his fans watched
from the sidelines.

The moment he won he swiveled around to kiss
his mom.
And then his friends piled on and threw their arms

around him and they all jumped up and down en masse.
I got up for the remote so I could hear his remarks.
Bendinelli said he'd been down and out but rose again.

Bendinelli said it was the best day of his life.
El mejor día de mi vida. Largest European Poker Tour
to date. The announcer said *All you need is a chip and a chair.*

And I'm off and running, thinking of other All you needs: *A fish
and a pole. A God and a religion. A poet and a rhyme.* They play
him off with a song: "I Get Knocked Out" by Smash Mouth.

Life and Other Maladies

If Mother Nature don't stop you, Father Time will.
—Brook Benton

Early in the morning Tom fell and hit his head on the router, and we are back again, hoping not to become regulars at Advanced Urgent Care on Arroyo Parkway. The main room is packed, so we sit in the kids' waiting room with the too-bright mural of a garden scene; Barney and Thomas the Tank Engine on TV. We can see through the doorway into the main waiting room where jungle footage is streaming on a large wall-mounted screen. Bright birds. At first I think it's Costa Rica. But the crocodiles bring Africa to mind. The woman across from us coughs violently through her mask. There must be nine patients or family groups ahead of us. When it's our turn we're called into the exam room. Dr. Miguel looks Tom over and says he'll be all right but needs stitches and a better story to explain the scar. Perhaps a skateboard accident or a showdown with an attacker. Who says we only die once? I have died a million times worrying about leaving the ones who still need me. You're never the same after that.

Meanwhile, daily dispatches from emergency services. What will it be today? Tsunami, high winds, wildfire, winter storm, earthquake, flash flood, civil war, government takeover? If you dislike surprises, don't live on the Ring of Fire. If LA is the frying pan, Tokyo is the fire. Mother Nature is keeping us on our toes in the lands of the Pacific Rim. Tonight there was a 7.1 in Western Japan. Little damage. We called right away. Nicky and Yuka are okay, thank God. A megaquake warning in place for the next week. The authorities are keeping an eye on Fukushima and a tsunami warning is in effect. It looks like a typhoon is heading their way. What are we supposed to do with all that?

The one we had here two weeks ago tonight registered 5.7 initially, downgraded to a 5.2. Epicenter somewhere outside Bakersfield. 9:09 p.m. I was eating cherries. Mimi (our cat) and I sensed something before we felt the twenty second rolling motion, so unlike the jolt and drop we used to feel at our old house. Here we're on an alluvial plain; there we were ten feet above bedrock.

We can see Mt. Wilson through the front window. *It's an earthquake, Mimi*, I said. *I'm glad you're here with me, kitty.* We were both more curious than afraid, although I did wake up in the night trembling the way you do when you have a fever, and my mind went to somatic experiencing class, where we learned animals don't carry trauma in their bodies because they know to shake it off.

Mimi must have felt it more than I, so close to the ground. She seemed as anxious for Pop to come home as I did and waited by the front door. He was teaching a night class on the other side of town. We say the other side of town, but by town we mean all of LA County. I was born here on the Eastside, lived for years on the Westside and now we're back where I started. Pop loves it. By Pop I mean my husband, Tom. At first our son called him Daddy, then Dad, then Pop and now Pops. I still call him Pop. He was expected home in forty minutes.

There were twenty-four imperceptible aftershocks in the first hour after it happened. They've drummed into us that an aftershock is sometimes foreshock to a monster quake. We ask our nephew for updates from the seismo lab at Caltech. He was part of a team sent to Iceland to fine-tune monitoring equipment before the volcano erupted in December. I went to school with Gail Richter, daughter of Charles Richter, father of the Richter scale. He came to speak to our fourth-grade class, but I can't remember one word.

The last one was a 4.6. Near South Pasadena. The windows shook for twenty seconds. We always rush to read about it. How strong? Epicenter? Damage? Facts offer the illusion of control. We check our flashlights and batteries, hand-crank and solar-powered radios and update our emergency plan. It's the most and least we can do.

IV

Two Cats in the Yard

—Graham Nash, "Our House"

First came Charlie, the little red cat, skin and bones at first, still lean and mean, our backyard Julius Caesar, a part of the family, named after my grandfather Charlie McCormick. He showed up on our back wall one day and took up residence in our affections.

Then came Smokey, the Norwegian Forest cat who coveted Charlie's food. At first they clashed but Smokey quickly became the loyal sidekick.

Soon there may be three, now that Gray comes around. Smokey goes nose to nose with Gray, doesn't mind his company. But Charlie, the reluctant Alpha, held out at first, put

on a show of protest before sharing his bowl. Now each cat has his own. Gray is solid and muscular, like a panther, with intense yellow eyes, intimidating at first. But now he nuzzles

our legs and purrs. They're the regulars. The founding fathers of the colony. George Washington, Thomas Jefferson, James Madison. Triumvirate of fur. Relishing their Sheba Perfect Portions and Blue Wilderness dry. But we know they're here for more than the food.

They must know we love them. They luxuriate in the beds of catmint we've planted, roll around ecstatically to absorb as much scent as they can. We talk endlessly about their interactions and their comings and goings. If we're not

outside they come and look for us at every door and greet us in the driveway when we've been away from home. Mimi lives inside.

She's a Ragdoll, named after my grandmother Williemarie (Mimi) McCormick. When we brought our kitty home we promised she'd be an indoor cat. My brother says cats think we're on a hunt when we're away and worry we'll be taken by larger predators. He says that's why they're so happy to see us when we return. He says cats bring us mice and birds to show us how it's done.

Cha Cha lives in the back house with the kids. Yuka named her.

We've since learned our outdoor cats have other names and homes. Charlie's first people called him Milo. When these neighbors moved two blocks away he chose to stay behind. They brought us his baby picture; said he's not two, as we'd guessed,

but eight, and legendary. He fought off a coyote, left a clump of grey coyote fur in the dust embedded with a few of his claws. Charlie's known by his new family as Shadow. They live in the house behind us on Maiden Lane.

The cat formerly known as Wimpy, after the character on Popeye, for his love of food, especially hamburgers, is the one we now call Smokey. He lives two doors up. Our friend Debra named her visiting cat Brisket but his real name is Stormy. Our neighbors like to name their cats all shades of gray. Shadow, Stormy, Smokey, Gray. Gray is a Russian Blue.

Charlie, our Huckleberry cat, is not mine. Like all the main men in my life—husband, son, father, brothers—he likes the comforts of home, but might light out for the territory if I try to *sivilize* him too hard. It's that combination of warmth and waywardness that draws me in. They must know by now. I'm a bit feral myself.

Poetry

We're all just walking each other home.
—Ram Dass

Dad was not a man of few words. He was a talker; a teller of jokes. He liked things to make sense. He was not a big reader, except for newspapers, but he loved words, crossword puzzles, limericks, song lyrics, plays on words, double-entendres. He could sit and read a dictionary for hours, for fun. He liked elevated words like *ancillary, matriculate, recalcitrant.* The youngest of four formidable boys, Dad was quiet early on. But words set him free. And now, after his first stroke, he was speaking poetry.

I guess I'm skating on the morte.

I'm roughing the bore.

Something snapped.

I got my brain straight.

I'm phasing out.

That's not the warning.

And then, gravely earnest:

I'm scripture.

A few weeks earlier, we made a trip to San Francisco, seven of us, to mark his eightieth birthday. A few weeks before that Dad fell while walking the dog in their neighborhood. At the time his doctor thought he was okay but at the very end of our journey, on a visit to the Natural History Museum in Golden Gate Park, Dad got a bad headache, first clue he'd developed a subdural hematoma when he fell and hit his head. The swelling precipitated the stroke and necessitated a craniotomy. It took some time for his words to come back. But they did.

His expressions had always been *tried and true*. Clichés to some, but poetry to me even then:

Nature's noblemen

Salt of the earth

God's country

We're not here by chance

Ho Hum, another day in paradise

Rock of Gibraltar

Pure unadulterated corn

Dad started his own company in his early thirties. He named it Power Plus. He transformed himself into a brilliant salesman of the products he and his brother invented: engine management systems, oil level regulators and the one he proudly called the *Smart Tank* long before phones and other machines were called smart. *You absolutely don't need this product,* he'd say to prospects. And they didn't. It worked like a charm. He made just about every sale.

When Dad got sober he learned a new language. The meetings, his fellows and the *Big Book* added volumes to his repertoire.

Acceptance is the key

Came to believe

Being a part of

God grant me the serenity

I can't but we can

Struck sober

Self-will run riot

Self-knowledge availed us nothing

The good news is, the war is over; the bad news is, we lost

Let go and Let God

Three years later, after the second stroke, he had the words straight in his head, for the most part, but struggled to form them with his mouth and make himself understood.

I rode with him in the ambulance from the hospital to Ocean View Convalescent Hospital in Encinitas and when we pulled up to the entrance it struck me hard. Dad would not be getting out of there alive. The lobby was decorated for the holidays with poinsettias, automated angels with golden curls, electric menorahs. I tried to stay cheerful but walking beside him on the gurney ride down the corridor to his room was bracing. A few days into the stay they moved Dad to a room with a distant ocean view. It wasn't a bad room. There was a sitting area when you walked in the door and another set of chairs, upholstered in a palm frond print, near the window next to the hospital bed. We could see the sunset from his room and at night the train rattled past and we could hear the crossing bells chime and the train whistle blow.

Dad lived another few weeks. This last stroke left him partially paralyzed on one side and he'd been in and out of the ICU at Scripps Encinitas in the last stages of kidney and heart failure. He was on a feeding tube since he could no longer swallow and required dialysis every other day. He had a terrible thirst and a parched mouth and we kept a supply of glycerine swabs by his bed and a cup of ice chips which we fed to him with a plastic spoon.

All he wanted was to go home and sit in the recliner with his old dog by his side. Bud, the black retriever mix with a white muzzle, successor to Sam, their beloved black and white Cocker Spaniel, who'd died not long before.

Every word was a project. Nine days before he died Dad felt great urgency to deliver a short message to the family. The dictation took a long, long time but I got it down and checked every word with him twice. What he wanted most to say was that he loved his wife and family very much and that it was difficult to have complete understanding and not be able to express himself.

One afternoon a few days before he died Dad turned to my sister and me—we were on opposite sides of the bed, each holding one of his hands—and said, with great difficulty, *I'm a lucky man.* We smiled at him and held back tears and then looked at each other. *I sure do love you kids,* he said. We weren't exactly kids. I was fifty. She was fifty-six.

He died peacefully about eight in the evening on January 10, 2000, his four kids by his side—my sister, two brothers and me. We held the memorial at his regular early-morning meeting at the Sixth Step House on Pacific Coast Highway. He was a much-loved elder by then in North County San Diego recovery circles, a seventeen-year veteran of the program. His fellows told stories of how he'd helped them, what he'd meant to them. A few of them said he'd saved their lives. When they met Dad one of them was without a home; one had just gotten out of prison; one was on the verge of suicide.

Dad's AA fellows loved his humor and his contradictions. He called himself a devout agnostic but always picked *The Lord's Prayer* when it was his turn to choose. He was known to have said more than once, *Thank God for the Chapter to the Agnostic!* He liked to have the last word, and when it came to the existence of God he was adamant in his position: *I just don't know.* But he did believe in a Higher Power. It was decidedly scriptural, and also paradoxical: *For where two or three are gathered in my name there am I among them (Matthew 18:20).*

Blind Faith

A poem begins as a lump in the throat, a sense of wrong, a homesickness, a lovesickness.
—Robert Frost

Sometimes I try to phone home, in dreams, and there is no phone; or I try to phone home and there is no home. Sometimes futile pleas for help. Empty stairwells, back alleys, junkyards and abandoned buildings. Sometimes a menacing stranger.

I ask my husband to play it again on YouTube. "Can't Find My Way Home." Did they know this anthem would speak to our collective angst? Ginger Baker's on drums in a green embroidered tunic. Clapton hadn't wanted to play the old Cream and Traffic songs, but this was one of the few that were new.

We see the Thames and the trees and the crowd of 100,000 fans. The band is on the outdoor stage at Hyde Park. June 7, 1969. Their first gig. Steve Winwood's on keys and at the microphone. *We're going to do a new number called . . .* The camera cuts to a shirtless guy wearing a headband and dreads, dancing freely in the crowd. Early June, 1969, I'm in Pasadena, learning my mother has just months to live.

How many times, decades later, did we watch that scene in *The Land Before Time,* my little son and I, looking at each other through tears. When the dying mother says, *I'll be in your heart, Littlefoot. Let your heart guide you.* Who on this earth has not felt as lonely as an orphan; has not yearned for home.

Mountain View

All four of my grandparents are buried here
and they are in good company.
My sister-in-law calls it their forever home,
just a mile from our house. I find strength
and comfort in their nearness.

It's one of the good ones, as cemeteries go,
and it lives up to its name, ringed on three sides
by the San Gabriel Mountains and in the shade
of giant deodars lining the avenues.

Octavia Butler rests here. Eldridge Cleaver.
Richard Feynman. George Reeves,
first TV Superman, who knew both
Mom and Dad at City College. George invited
Mom to cut class and watch a movie
but she declined. In an unrelated incident
Superman was knocked out
by Dad in boxing class.

Williemarie Hannon, my mother's mother,
was flirtatious, loyal, beautiful,
romantic, respected in business.
Charlie McCormick, my mother's father,
was sociable and funny, beloved and charismatic.

Florence Hammond, my father's mother,
was spiritual, literary, practical, loving, thrifty,
forgiving and free-thinking; a suffragette
and a warrior for women's reproductive rights.
Edmund Nelson, my father's father, was hardworking
and fun-loving; serious and formidable.

Before he died he told us he'd done everything
in his life he'd wanted to do. I was fourteen and I
fortified myself with Shakespeare:

This thou perceivs't which makes thy love grow strong,
to love that well which thou must leave e'er long.

I take after my grandparents. I'm plain and fancy,
frivolous and serious, hardworking, fun-loving;
capricious (given to sudden or unaccountable
changes of mood or behavior) and sensible
(wise, prudent); fearful and brave; full of doubt
and full of faith. Like every human, a quandary
of contradictions; equation of hurt and resilience;
answer to the ardor of generations.

Until recently I was quite sure I wanted to be scattered at sea,
like my father, like my father-in-law and mother-in-law before
me. Become one with salt water; be everywhere at once; rain down

over Kansas or roll up on the sands of Okinawa. Because I find
my beloveds in the wind and light, flowers and trees; in the rocks,
oceans and rivers, planets and stars and the spaces between;
the butterfly on my shoulder. I guess I'll let the others decide.

When we brought Willie here—my siblings and I—
Williemarie—we visited the others. Edmund, Florence,
Charlie; his mother, Emma Louise, and younger brother, Bob.
Mom left us young and wanted to be buried up north
with Gee Gee, our great-grandmother.

Dad's send-off was the most dramatic. He didn't care what we did with the ashes. He told my stepmother. we could flush them down the toilet for all he cared. Instead we chartered a boat.

Once we were far enough from land and in deep enough waters off the coast at Oceanside our cousin Bill did the honors. Dad's favorite nephew. He scattered the ashes and each of us tossed in a long-stemmed rose.

I can't remember which of my brothers noticed it first. Once the ashes hit the water they didn't spread apart as we thought they would but floated closer together to form what looked like the shape of a person on the surface of the water. We sang *Allá en el Rancho Grande,* Dad's favorite, and *Amazing Grace.* Right about then the dolphins appeared, an unmistakable real-life pod of them, in case there was any doubt.

A Long Way to Rarotonga

Last time in paradise
we saw birds with red crests,
ocean palms, plumeria blossoms,
grass houses with low-pitched
roofs in the island style.
There was a rainbow, to taunt us.
I recorded a bird chorus
on my phone one morning
on the balcony;
a call and response concerto
of whoops, chirps, twitters and caws.
Scent of plumeria on the cool breeze.
Hypnotized by the sunset beauty,
not watching where I was going
I stepped on a fire ant hill on our way back
from the beach at dusk. It took months
for the stings to heal.
We are planning a trip
in honor of big birthdays
and a historic anniversary.
I'm looking for peace. I'd like
to feel the way I did that day
in the pool at Hana with the ones I love.
Calm, comfortable, relaxed. The water
perfect, the air
soft, the wind in the palms
lovely and soothing.
But a day like that

can't be willed into being. Some days
are fire ants, start to finish. Travelers
on YouTube rhapsodize and advise.
How to navigate the breakfast
buffet. Whether to get an overwater
bungalow. Sunburned honeymooners,
intrepid elders, island footage
and close-ups of black pearls
from the night market,
Will it be the Cook Islands
or French Polynesia? I always
thought I wanted to go.
Haven't we traveled enough
for one lifetime? Only other
place I really want to be is Japan
with the kids.

When the Light Breaks Over You

—after Seamus Heaney

Because you told us so, I see you as a boy,
Seamus Heaney, your father digging
in the boggy soil as you handle the cold
potatoes; walk in the wake of his footsteps,
wanting *to grow up and plough.* Because you
told us so I know you loved wells and their turbid
smell; *dipping and drinking* with your hands;
and how the blackbirds in St. Kevin's hand
are *fledged and flown.* How words like *coeval,
heft, hatched, and honeyed* roost in your poems. Coyotes
and bobcats dwell in the parched hills where I live.
But today I think of greener pastures. I think
of Sweeney *and the soft conversation of the turtledoves,
the blackbirds' song, the stag upon the hill, the howl
of the wolf pack.* How you never felt closer to your mother
than with your head leaning in towards hers over a bowl
of cool water, peeling potatoes *while the others were
at Mass.* I was too preoccupied to take in your greatness
when you came to speak at my college. Children and elders
know best how to dig—you; and Williemarie McCormick,
my grandmother, knees to the ground planting pansies
and petunias in the hard California soil; and Kitty, Kristin
and I—kindergarten fugitives of the pinecone gang—
digging in the schoolyard to tree roots that smelled
of sassafras.

Maybe You Can Go Home Again

Maybe it takes years for you to return
and it's not altogether rosy when you do

but you're better now with contradictions
and the tribulation can't eclipse the jubilation.

Maybe you hear your mother's song
as you drive along the streets of town:

I'll be seeing you in all the old familiar places.
Maybe sea beasts

and rocky waters kept you away or Sirens
sang you off-course. Maybe you moved away

not long after she died. Maybe Dorothy was right,
and there is no place like home. Maybe you can go home,

over and over again, to tall palms and blue mountains;
raucous squawk of rogue parrots; orange blossom air;

carpet of acorns and oak leaves. Maybe home is a prayer.

Unrule This Ruly Paradise

Purple of penstemon, bright yellow
of desert marigold; low-hanging fruit,
ensorcelled by light. We couldn't tame it
if we tried. Scent
of sage and apricot-colored
roses. Buzz of bees, love affair
of lavender and lilac,
aubergine and violet. I can't remember
a Spring that's smelled this sweet.
Low hum
of hummingbird, warble and wing-song
of doves when they're startled
and take flight.
Taste of oranges from the hundred-year-old
tree. Rough of the wooden bench.
Sweet ring of chimes.
Faded opulence
of the ripened rose, pale
Isabella Segunda blue.
Stray branch of star jasmine.
Little butterflies, pygmy blue and fiery skipper.
Channel Islands poppy. How can you not
love this world?
We've had rain, this year and last,
long overdue,
and the hills are green.

Some things do live up
to your wildest dreams. Wild lilac
and desert willow. The Mississippi.
The Sphinx. A perfect peach.
Sex. Love. Your precious child.
Your own backyard.

About the Author

A third-generation Californian, Lin Nelson Benedek lives with her husband Tom in Altadena and wrote these poems under the spell of wildflowers, orange blossoms, and the San Gabriel Mountains. A longtime psychotherapist, Lin is passionate about the importance of human connection and believes in the power of poetry to heal, connect, and enchant us.

Lin earned her MFA in Writing at Pacific University in Forest Grove, Oregon. She has poems published in numerous journals, seven anthologies, and three previous full-length collections: *I Was Going to Be a Cowgirl* (2017); *When a Peacock Speaks to You in a Dream* (2018); and *Singing Lessons* (2020), all published by Kelsay Books. Lin is now working on new poems for a chapbook about the Eaton Fire and its aftermath. She recently completed revisions on a memoir called *Love-Starved Girl*.

www.ingramcontent.com/pod-product-compliance
Lightning Source LLC
Chambersburg PA
CBHW071010160426
43193CB00012B/1999